ABANDONED

By the same author
Fragments: Echo of the Past.

ABANDONED
A Life of Shadows

KATE TAYLOR

Cover photo: ©*Alone* by Cherie Wren
Illustration: ©*Silhouette of a girl with flowing hair* by Vlada Grechko

National Library of New Zealand Cataloguing-In-Publication Data

Taylor, Kate
Abandoned : a life of shadows / Kate Taylor
ISBN 978-0-473-25337-0
I. Title.
NZ821.3—dc 23

CONTENTS

INTRODUCTION

During my life's struggle, I couldn't find anything that I could really relate to, where I felt truly understood or known. So I decided to write my own thoughts down, uncensored, never intending them to be seen by anyone else.

Now I'm realising that I don't have to be ashamed or fearful or guilty for having such a dark secret world and I don't need to hide it either.

If you are suffering too, never give in, never give up. My depression and anxiety began as a child and it's all I've known — if I can hang in there, so can you. You are not alone.

Mental Health is Truth.

A LIFE LESS LIVED

I crave a life, less lived
Free from the old ideas
That cling like mildew
Inhibiting independence
Reducing potential
Limiting range of motion

Free from feeling
Continually drained
By the constant effort
Required to maintain
And perform
A worn out role

Where the days are not
Routinely recycled
Echoes of the past
Inducing
A perpetual stagnation
At the expense of growth

Living life moment to moment
Where the sun's warmth
Can be truly felt
Not just appreciated
As the conceptual entity
It often seems to be.

ABANDONED

Don't you see my wounds

Red
Raw
Oozing

In front of you

How can you turn away
And leave me alone

Slowly bleeding to death
Drowning in pools
Of my own blood

Where are you?

ALONE

I awaken alone
Aching
With remembrance
That you have left me
Immersed in grief
Coldly abandoned

Time moves slowly
This silence deafens
Clarity is lost
In shades of grey
My cries fading
In the nothingness

Remaining
The desperate longing
For salvation
Helplessly waiting
As I drown
In the absence of you

Regretful
That I compromised
So much of myself
Leaving behind
This bitter taste
Of wasted sacrifice.

BETRAYED

I trusted in you
To hold some of my pain
For a while I let you see
Beneath the surface

Now when I see you
You look the other way
Leaving me on my own
To regret my decision

I should have known
That you were only pretending
So you could feel better
About your own life

Pretentious self-important fraud
How petty and small minded
I hope one day you realise
How hurtful it is

Awaking to find yourself
Alone and betrayed
By someone you thought cared
With no sympathy from me.

BLACK

Through the violence and despair
I curled up tight
And hid from sight
Small, cold, alone, scared

Alive
Inside
Alive
To hear the pounding rhythm
And feel the damp tears

So alive
Inside
A piece of me
Uncompromised
Unbroken
Buried in black

You killed all
But that part of me
You thought
The corpse was yours
But you were stupid to think

I'D EVER BELONG TO SOMEONE ELSE!

BLIND

Being blind at the time
Of deception

Simply means

That when the light
Eventually dawns

It takes longer
To work through
The faulty veil of memory

To reconcile the truth
With the experience.

DIE QUIETLY

For too long I hid myself away
From view, from myself
The voice of the angry critic
Constantly in my head

Now at the verge of freedom
The beginning of self expression
You deny me your friendship
As you drown in angry bitterness

Preferring me to lie down in a corner
Away from view and quietly die.

ECLIPSE

I rage at the sun
For shining so bright
Leaving me lost in shadow
Lost in the dark

Alone I descend to Hell
A place too familiar
A place in mind
But the body remembers it too

I dread this eclipse
It frightens me
It happens so suddenly
I forget I am only visiting

I am so grateful
That you are here
To care, to remind me
It is not my life now

You see courage in my struggle
Strength in my tears
Through your eyes I feel less freakish
More substantial

Your view gives me a validity
That I never thought possible —
You see me
And you don't run

You even encourage me
To be more myself
To write, to express the world
I am not able to voice

Who could have ever imagined
Such a blessing could happen to me
In my world of shadow
You are the light that leads the way.

FALLEN

I lie here numb
Fallen at your feet
Gasping for breath
Struggling with the wounds
You so carelessly inflicted

Your accumulated actions
Finally claiming their prize
But you are no longer here
My struggle does not amuse
And you have better things to do

This clarity hurts
Permeating the very marrow
Of these wary bones
I am unloved, unacknowledged
Unseen and uncared for

Brokenly drowning in despair
Lost to the dark
I long for the release
And the sweet freedom
That comes with death.

FIGHT

Time does not heal all wounds
That's what you thought though
When you let me slip away
You hoped with time I would forget

You assumed I wouldn't last
That I wasn't strong enough
To stand tall by myself
And be my own person

That humbled by your absence
I would come running back
Having learnt my lesson
Eager to please again

You were so very naive
To think that I would ever
Return to captivity
After a taste of freedom

Freedom that came with a cost
But it is a worthy fight
Failure is not an option
When you're never going back

And now I have a greater
Understanding of who I am
With no need to apologise
For living my own life.

GOODBYE

How do I say goodbye to you
I don't even know where to begin
I can't find the strength to tell you
All you mean to me
I just hope you know I care
And that as I move forward in life
All I do, everything that follows
Comes from me knowing you

You have given me reasons to continue living
You have replaced my despair with calm
My despondency with hope
And my fears with faith

You are the prism through which light travels
The moisture through which a rainbow forms
And the presence through which
I move about in the world

You are my blessing.

HOPE?

My memories are constant
Relentlessly unforgiving
Uninviting and ever present
A life time of despondency
Burrowed beneath the surface

A river of unshed tears
A never ending void
Filled with lost hopes and dreams
Reluctantly abandoned
When reality did not comply

I have lingered so long
In this place of damnation
That sometimes I wonder
If I will be forever trapped —
If leaving is even possible

New remembrances are made
From times now more enjoyable
But the past is always there
Unseen but continually felt
Pressing in on the present

I am regularly drowning and drained
Constantly fighting to stay afloat
With little residual energy
To motivate or inspire —
Prolonging the process of change.

IGNORANCE

What have you done to me
That makes me descend
To unfathomable depths
To live a frightened
And terrified existence
To wish to die
To feel like dying
To die
Over and over again
How dare you deny my pain
(Your pain)
How dare you ridicule my tears
Love it's not what you know
You kill me with your ignorance.

LOST

I feel so wrong
Everyone around me
Seems to shine
And I feel so dull

Uneasily put together
Bundles of pain
Randomly joined
Like a patchwork quilt

So disjointed
So ungainly
I awkwardly falter
Through a haphazard life

Never feeling like I fit in
Always hiding inside
The endless sorrow
That never leaves

A lifetime of stumbling
Around in the dark
Clumsy and uncoordinated
Trying to act like I belong.

NO HISTORY

I long to be more
To have the freedom
To move unselfconsciously
And confidently
Through a richer life

To not dwell wearily
On the pain of the past
To be free of despair
To live outside of time
Irrespective of history

To be all I am
Not who I could have been
Fulfilling new dreams
No longer weighted down
By a worn out perspective

No more lamentations
About unused potential
Or mourning for a future
Based on past ideologies
That no longer apply.

NO RESPECT

Your familiarity imposes
Upon my sense of self
Restricting freedom
You imagine you know me

Having this impression
You take liberties
With reduced sensitivity
Leaving respect behind.

NUMB

I feel where your fingernails
Have raked across my heart
You tried to erase my life
My hope
Leaving behind a darkness
That penetrated my soul

So cold

So black
So quiet
So alone

I can't even hear the sound
Of my tears
All is lost to this numbness
And like a mechanical robot
I go on and on

But for how much longer?

OUTER / INNER

Outside the night arrives
To cover the day
Clarity is lost
Leaving shadow and shape
Indistinguishable now

Inside a similar
Lack of distinction
Smothers our perception
Reducing definition
Leaving vagueness to prevail

This mirroring of worlds
Means solace can be found
In a tiny hummingbird
Or a breaking wave:
Nature as medicine.

PATRIARCHY

Rigidly unwavering
Your view is inflexible
A world of ordered soldiers
Your version of utopia

No freedom of expression — "You're all wrong"
No art — "What a waste of time"
No music — "It's not like it was in my day"
No movies — "Too much swearing anyway"

I am the only point of view you need to have.

PLEASING

Some people are impossible to please
Because they don't find you pleasing
Every step to gain their approval
Is a step away from yourself
Until you have sold your soul
For a handful of careless praises
Which slip through outstretched fingers
Leaving behind a being drenched in remorse.

REFLECTION

I am not who I was
Who you wanted me to be
Who you expect me to be
An illusion, a forgery

The mime that looks
Into the mirror
But cannot see
Herself looking back

And she is confused
By the superimposed image
Familiarity withheld
Reflecting an imposter

Anger rises quietly
As it begins to dawn
The wounds are self imposed
And she has sold herself out

All so others may feel
More at ease in her presence
Allowing her to remain hidden
At home in the dark

Afraid to be seen or heard
Or to be known
Fearing the recriminations
That haunt from the past

Only now it's not enough
Tired of holding herself down
Holding herself back
Of being less

Tired of the death mask
With its plastic smile
Accompanied by inane politeness
Long past its use by date

Resentful of those
That seek to diminish
Who prefer she never shine
Or rage or change or Be

NO MORE — I can't stand it
NO MORE — I'm dying inside
NO MORE — It's not enough
NO MORE — It's never enough.

RELEASE

I feel numb
Slowly drowning
Lost in memories
I wish I didn't have

The bliss of surrender
The relief of never having
To hold on again
To die — to be free

No more panic attacks
No more recriminations
No more living an empty
Meaningless life

No more chills
As repressed visions
Surface to steal
The light

To never have to mourn
For a single lost moment
The absence of love or joy or hope
To be whole

Free to embrace whatever
Is presently in front of me
The strength and delight
Of standing on my own.

SHADOWS

How do I relate to a world
That does not know what lies
Burning beneath the surface
The pain behind the smile

My edges too sharp to fit
Contentedly into your world
Appearing aloof
An enigmatic stranger

Yet you are aware of more
Than first impressions imply
At the brink of perception
The outline of something larger

But that is enough for you
You don't try to see more
You would rather not know
About the shadows where I live.

SURRENDER / ECLIPSE 2

I rage at the sun
It shines so bright
Leaving me
Lost in shadow
Lost in the dark

I dread this eclipse
It's so sudden
Frightening me
Devouring me
Reclaiming me

So cold this descent
It feels like hell
Dragging me
Back down again
Alone again

So black, this endless night
It never ends
Draining me
This constant fight
This place in mind

Longing for release
It's so tempting
Calling me
Serenity
In surrender.

SURVIVOR

Death my elusive friend
Who has walked beside me
For the longest time
My only companion
On the darkest of days

And on the blackest nights
When light cannot be found
At the heart of pain
Forsaken and alone
I find myself at home

Abandoned long ago
I had forgotten
That rather than disappear
I chose to exist here
On the outside, hidden

As I move on with life
I find myself conflicted
With what is presented
And the way of surviving
I have learned to become.

THANK YOU

Your melodic words
Fill me with a longing
To be able to self express
With such clarity and beauty

I hear your soulful phrases
And they gladden me
Because I realise
That through you I am known

Your expression frees me
It gives me the belief
That I can find my voice
And it will be appreciated

Your music shows me
That singing about the dark
Is not only valid
It is freedom

The demons in the shadows
Can never be faced
If you are too afraid
To shine a light

Thank you for your light
For being brave enough
To reveal your pain
It frees us both.

THE CAUSE

Why did I ever let
You take away my words
My point of view
My self-expression
My way of making
Sense of the world

You violated my trust
Trespassing on my right
To privacy
Smothering creativity
In a vain attempt
To reduce individuality

Like a moth in a jar
You played with my efforts
To evolve myself
Preferring me to suffocate
Than fly away
Fulfilling my own destiny

So many years spent trying
To find the voice I lost
Wondering why you would want
Me to be less —
To be such a shadow
Of who I really am

Just beginning to see
How lost you truly were
How the painful fragments
Of your jagged past
Could reflect such
A distorted image

Such a shame then
That you didn't think
To spare me the same fate
How can you see the effect
But distance yourself
From the cause?

THE SACRIFICE

I don't know why
I chose to be so closed
About the way
I saw the world to be

Why I was so afraid
To see what shadows
Would appear
If I stepped into the light

Thinking it better
To stay in the dark
Where no one could see
The failure I had become

Not realising the pain
Was not all mine to bear
That I was carrying
Yours as well

Too much responsibility
For a little girl to hold
Drowning in the tears
You cried on my shoulder

Confused and conflicted
Questioning sanity
Constantly struggling
To maintain perspective

When coldly you turned away
Leaving me alone to grieve
For the mother I sacrificed
My childhood for.

THE VIEW

I'm slowly fading away
Time is so unkind
Memories refusing
To release their hold
Dragging me down again

Can't stop myself from sinking
The way I've done before
The chains that bind
Too heavy to resist
And I'm too weary to try

I see I've held on so tight
To who I thought I should be
Freedom confined
By invisible shackles
That mould and enslave unseen

The view is so clear
Here beneath the surface
Immersed in silence
Removed from context
The clarity of drowning.

YOU WERE WRONG

I saw through your facade
Of fictitious politeness
You use to camouflage
The claws you thought
Were too sharp to be seen

You mistakenly thought
You could repeatedly
Perfect your attacks
At my expense
And I would remain benign

You belatedly realised
You had forced things
You tried to change them back
You really thought
You could play me twice

Now daily you sit
And lament your injustice
In my face
Gaining strength from sympathy
Thinking to diminish me

It bothered me at first
Until I realised
You were out of my life
And I was really glad
To be my own person again.

ACKNOWLEDGMENTS

I wish to thank the following New Zealand organisations for their invaluable support:

GROW New Zealand Inc
www.grow.org.nz

Home and Family Counselling
www.homeandfamily.org.nz

Inner City Women's Group
www.innercitywomensgroup.org.nz

School of Philosophy (Auckland)
www.philosophy.school.nz

SPCA Auckland
www.spca.org.nz

The Salvation Army
www.salvationarmy.org.nz

Toi Ora Live Art Trust
www.toiora.org.nz